CHOIR CRACKUPS

The Church Musician's Book of Humor

Compiled by
John Yarrington

ABINGDON PRESS
Nashville, Tennessee

CHOIR CRACKUPS:
THE CHURCH MUSICIAN'S BOOK OF HUMOR

Copyright © 1999 by Abingdon Press

This book is printed on acid-free, recycled paper.

ISBN 0-687-08235-8

99 00 01 02 03 04 05 06 07 08 — 10 9 8 7 6 5 4 3 2 1

MANUFACTURED IN THE UNITED STATES OF AMERICA

BULLETIN BLOOPERS

The pastor will preach his farewell message, after which the choir will sing "Break Forth into Joy."

At the evening service tonight, the sermon topic will be "What Is Hell?" Come early and listen to our choir practice.

FOR BETTER OR FOR WORSE

"I THINK IT'S TIME WE ALL PITCHED IN AND BOUGHT THE CHOIR SOME CLASSIER-LOOKING ROBES."

BULLETIN BLOOPERS

Eight new choir robes are currently needed, due to the addition of several new members and the deterioration of some older ones.

BULLETIN BLOOPERS

 tewardship Offertory:
"Jesus Paid It All"

Haydn's Chopin Liszt at Vivaldi's

♫ Rossini and cheese

♫ Satie mushrooms

♫ Orange Schubert

♫ TchaiCOUGHsky drops

♫ Mozart-rella cheese

♫ I can't believe it's not Rutter

♫ New door Handel

♫ Little Debussy snack cakes

usic: A complex organization of sounds that is set down by the composer, incorrectly interpreted by the conductor, who is ignored by the musicians, the result of which is ignored by the audience.

FUNKY WINKERBEAN

Tom Batiuk

VOCABULARY

Music sung by two people at the same time is called a "duel."

I know what a "sextet" is, but I'd rather not say.

VOCABULARY

Perfect pitch: The smooth coating on a freshly paved road.

Bach chorale: The place behind the barn where you keep the horses.

MOTHER GOOSE & GRIMM **Mike Peters**

VOCABULARY

**ar line:** A gathering of people, usually among which may be found a church musician or two.

**ibrato:** Used by singers to hide the fact that they are on the wrong pitch.

Refrain: Refrain means, "Don't do it." A refrain in music is the part you better not try to sing.

VOCABULARY

Tenors: Most choirs have either a) none, or b) too many. When wholly absent they leave an aching void. When too numerous, they fill the void without removing the ache. Tenors rarely sing words and often produce regional sensations rather than actual notes. During the mating season, they draw attention to themselves by a practice known as "rubato."

© 1994 Universal Press Syndicate

Things for the Choir Director to Say When Caught Sleeping in a Staff Meeting

♫ They told me at the blood bank this might happen.

♫ I wasn't sleeping. I was meditating on our mission statement and envisioning a new paradigm.

♫ This is one of the seven habits of highly effective people.

♫ Someone must have put decaf in the wrong pot.

♫ Ah, the unique and unpredictable circadian rhythms of the workaholic.

♫ I wasn't sleeping! I was trying to pick up my contact lens without using my hands.

♫ Amen.

LITTLE KNOWN FACTS

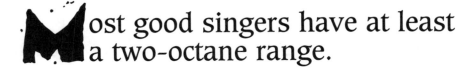**M**ost good singers have at least a two-octane range.

When they were not busy singing music, friars were short-order cooks in monasteries.

Accidentals: Wronng notes.

BULLETIN BLOOPERS

Today's Sermon: "How Much Can a Man Drink" with hymns from a full choir.

"Rev. Peterson is in the Holy Land, the youth pastor's under the church bus, and the minister of music is in jail for photocopying music. Want to talk to the janitor?"

HYMNS

The Politician's Hymn: "Standing on the Promises"

The Dentist's Hymn: "Crown Him with Many Crowns"

HYMNS

If you must speed on the highway:

45 mph	"God Will Take Care of You"
55 mph	"Guide Me, O Thou Great Jehovah"
65 mph	"Nearer, My God, to Thee"
75 mph	"Nearer, Still Nearer"
85 mph	"This World Is Not My Home"
95 mph	"Lord, I'm Coming Home"
100 mph	"Precious Memories"

"Let's sing that old favorite hymn 131 . . . with each of us altering the third stanza to suit his or her own views on the Millennium."

HYMNS

The IRS Hymn: "I Surrender All"

The Gossip's Hymn: "Pass It On"

The Optometrist's Hymn: "Open My Eyes That I May See"

Choir Proficiency Test

Question 1

You are in a choir processional and suddenly trip on your robe and fall down. You should:

    a. Assume a kneeling position and break into fervent prayer.

    b. Pretend that you've had a heart attack.

    c. Crawl into the nearest pew.

    d. Begin speaking in tongues.

(Answer on page 65)

Choir Proficiency Test

Question 2

While singing, you discover that the librarians have provided only one page of a two-page response. You should:

    a. Hum for your life.

    b. Sing "watermelon, watermelon, watermelon."

    c. Improvise an obbligato to sing on "oo."

    d. Try to get a hymnal out of the pew rack with your foot.

(Answer on page 65)

Choir Proficiency Test

Question 3

You are conducting the choir and orchestra in a very important performance, when suddenly you lose your grip and hurl the baton into the audience. You should:

    a. Grab the cellist's bow and proceed with aplomb.

    b. Without acknowledging the loss, coolly continue and occasionally flex the invisible baton to drive everyone mad.

    c. Inform the impaled individual that you have a piece of the rock.

    d. Signal for the custodian to turn on the lights while you crawl about in search of the baton.

(Answer on page 65)

Choir Proficiency Test

Question 4

You are a choir member who shows up late for service. You should:

    a. Climb into the back row of the choir loft from the organ chamber.

    b. Read M. Stephen's pamphlet, "Techniques for Tardy Appearances."

    c. Become hysterical in the choir room.

    d. Enter pretending to be a sound technician checking cables and then subtly insert yourself into the choir.

(Answer on page 65)

Choir Proficiency Test

Question 5

The person sharing your music in rehearsal had a garlic tamale for dinner. You should:

    a. Complain of lack of air, then grab your throat and fall convulsed on the floor while muttering "garlic, ugh, garlic!"

    b. Pass the offender a hymnal open to "Purify Me, Lord."

    c. Sing without inhaling.

    d. Say, "I detect garlic tamale on your breath. Do you have a recipe for that?"

(Answer on page 65)

Choir Proficiency Test

Question 6

Inevitably that dreaded big sneeze occurs toward the end of "Still, Still, Still." You should:

    a. As you sneeze, come down hard on your neighbor's instep to create a diversion.

    b. Cram your stole into your mouth to muffle the noise.

    c. Try to make it harmonize.

    d. Doesn't really matter, because the director is going to kill you anyway.

(Answer on page 65)

SONGLINES

While traveling in Australia, author Bruce Chatwin discovered to his amazement that Aboriginal tribes could trace and map the territory they journeyed by musical intonations they memorized that paralleled the contours of the land. These intonations were expressed as "songlines" in his book of the same name, which proved sufficient to lead them back to places they might not have returned to in some time. I like to think of the pieces of music that I love as songlines of my life. They return me to memory and guide me to places I still need to explore.

Sir, you have been recommended for our remedial singing class that meets in the basement of our annex.

VOCABULARY

Whole note: What's due after failing to pay the mortgage for a year.

Accent: An unusual manner of pronunciation, for example: "Y'all sang real good!"

Harmony: A corn-like food eaten by people with accents (see above for definition of "accent").

VOCABULARY

Syncopation: A condition incurred from lack of roughage in one's diet.

Transsectional: An alto who moves to the soprano section.

Relative minor: The child of a music teacher.

THE ORGAN

The organ is the instrument of worship—for in its sounding we sense the majesty of God, and in its ending we know the grace of God.

WHEN CHOIR DIRECTORS DREAM.

THE ORGAN

Feet: Many organists make use of both of these. Generally, the left one is in charge of vibrations, while the right cruises gently in sympathy. A good organist does little damage with the right foot.

Prayer of Confession for Choir Members

Almighty and most merciful Conductor,
We have erred and strayed from thy beat like lost sheep;
We have followed too much the intonations and tempi of our own hearts.
We have offended against thy dynamic markings.
We have left unsung those notes that we ought to have sung,
And we have sung those notes that we ought not to have sung.
And there is no support in us.

But thou, O Conductor, have mercy upon us, miserable singers;
Succor the chorally challenged;
Restore them that need sectionals;
Spare thou them that have no pencils.
Pardon our mistakes, and have faith that hereafter we will follow
Thy directions and sing together in perfect harmony.

"We are happy to announce that in spite of our reduced budget, we are still able to afford a church organist."

HYMNS

The Best of Country-Western Hymns

♫ "Been Roped and Thrown by Jesus in the Holy Ghost Corral"

♫ "Drop Kick Me, Jesus, Through the Goalposts of Life"

♫ "Thank God and Greyhound She's Gone"

REV

LITTLE KNOWN FACTS

If you took all the tenors in the world and laid them end to end—it would be a good idea.

HYMNS

The Tailor's Hymn: "Holy, Holy, Holy"

The Electrician's Hymn: "Send Out Thy Light"

The Shopper's Hymn: "Sweet By and By"

BULLETIN BLOOPERS

The third verse of "Blessed Assurance" will be sung without musical accomplishment.

I think our church is on the verge of renewal—they wanted to sing the third verse of a hymn last Sunday!

OUT OF THE MOUTHS OF BABES

Handel was half-German, half-Italian, and half-English. He was rather large.

Question: Who composed the "Hallelujah" chorus?

Answer: God.

OUT OF THE MOUTHS OF BABES

John Sebastian Bach died from 1750 to the present.

My favorite carol is "Old Cumalye Faithful." Old Cumalye Faithful was Jesus' dog.

"I see we're running a little long this morning. For our final hymn, let's just sing every other word."

GLASBERGEN

OUT OF THE MOUTHS OF BABES

Just about any animal skin can be stretched over a frame to make a pleasant sound once the animal is removed.

Handel was a deeply religious man because in some of his music he talks about Ye and Thee and people like that.

VOCABULARY

Hymns: There are two kinds, long and short. They are bound together in volumes that are either too big or too little. Both kinds are sensitive to the pull of gravity at solemn moments.

Cipher: This is when a note on the organ refuses to stop.

VOCABULARY

Absence: The only quality of an organist that is generally recognized.

Recital: This is usually a performance given by the organist, with heavy emphasis on the word "given."

As we sing the 314th verse of "Just as I Am," isn't there *ONE MORE* who will come?

VOCABULARY

CUT TIME:.
   a. Parole.
   b. When everyone else is
      playing twice as fast as
      you are.

VOCABULARY

D.C. al Fine: Famous French composer.

Repeat sign: Graffiti that appears more than once on the blackboard. Erase immediately.

VOCABULARY

Metronome: A city-dwelling dwarf.

Modulation: Represents the Golden Mean: "Do everything in modulation."

VOCABULARY

Compound meter: A place to park your car that requires two dimes.

Duple meter: May take any even number of coins.

Triple meter: Only rich people should park by these.

VOCABULARY

Intervals
a. Major interval: A long time.
b. Minor interval: A few bars.
c. Inverted interval: When you have to go back a bar and try again.

Preparatory beat: A threat made to singers: "Sing, or else!"

BULLETIN BLOOPERS

The Senior Choir invites any member of the congregation who enjoys sinning to join the choir.

A songfest was hell at the Methodist Church Wednesday.

SCANDAL ROCKED THE MAPLE VALLEY CHURCH WHEN IT WAS DISCOVERED THAT THE CHOIR HAD BEEN LIP-SYNCING FOR THE LAST SIX YEARS.

OUT OF THE MOUTHS OF BABES

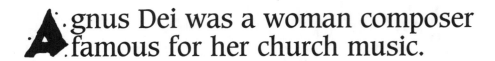 **A**gnus Dei was a woman composer famous for her church music.